Table of Contents: How to Succeed in th

Foreword by Roz McCarthy, Founder & CEO of Minorities for Medica
Introduction: How to Use this Workbook by Dasheeda Dawson 8

Part 1 Roles in the Legal Cannabis Industry	18
Cultivator / Grower	19
Parallels in History: the Gold Rush	21
Opportunities within Cannabis	25
Picks & Shovels Roles: Contractor or Consultant	27
Top Roles in the Cannabis Industry	29
How to Enter the Cannabis Industry	31
Part 2 Sectors in the Legal Cannabis Industry	39
Genetics	40
Seeds	41
Clones	42
Tissue Culture	43
Cultivation	45
Nursery	47
Sun Grown	49
Lamp Grown	50
Organic	52
Processing & Extractions	56
Extraction	60
Formulation	63
Delivery Mechanisms	66
Infusion	70
Veterinary	73
Packaging	75
Software & Information Technology	80
Marketing	83
Event Marketing	85
Content Marketing	86
Influencer Marketing	89
Retail	91
Tourism	93
Events	97
Sales & Distribution	100
Real Estate	104
Insurance	107
Human Resources	109
Legal	111
Education	114
Conclusion	117
Questions?	119

Foreword from **Roz McCarthy,**
Founder and CEO of Minorities for Medical Marijuana

In just a moment, I'm going to introduce you to a simple and unique method that can bring you more opportunities and wealth over the next 12-18 months, than most people will see in their entire careers.

What you're about to discover is a new and very different strategy that will help you create generational wealth, regardless; of how much money you currently have, the amount of formal education, or the background and skills you possess.

A bold statement, I know.

The secret behind this method is in the novel strategy that will put you in the center of the Green Rush. This is one of the fastest growing industries in our generation due to impending legalization, which turns other people's desires for a result into intense demand for you, whether it's your specific products or services. In fact, as you'll see it works with, or without, people who don't have insider connections or massive amounts of capital.

What you're about to discover is not theory. It's the strategy pioneered by Dasheeda Dawson, and what members of the J.A.R.V.I.Z. team have taught to hundreds of their students. These students have used this method to successfully enter the Green Rush, and set themselves up for getting a piece of the generational wealth being created by legalization. We will introduce several of these folks to you later.

This has nothing to do with any new whizbang money making tactics. It has nothing to do with any kind of newfangled MLM scheme. And it has nothing to do with the latest trend or fad.

Instead; the method outlined in this book, the 'picks and shovels' strategy gets you into the Green Rush with minimum risk and plenty of upside. The secret is focusing on non-plant touching opportunities, which allows you to succeed without having to risk engaging in any activities that are potentially illegal, without having massive capital or insider connections, and without worrying about getting scammed, robbed or ruined.

This is the golden age of cannabis. It's a time when the perceived risk is high. But; the actual risk is really much lower, and so there's this wonderful opportunity to find deals with relatively low valuations. And, perhaps not all of them, but some of them, are really going to take off...

I'm Roz McCarthy, Founder and CEO of Minorities for Medical Marijuana.

Minorities for Medical Marijuana, Inc (M4MM) is a non-profit organization with corporate offices based in Orlando, Florida. The organization is structured as a 501c3, with a full executive team and board of directors, who support the organization's overall global goals and strategic direction.

Minorities for Medical Marijuana is committed to cultivating a culturally inclusive environment where diversity of thought, experience and opportunities are valued, respected, appreciated and celebrated. M4MM serves as a resource to the community by providing information, referrals, advocacy, coordination, and education regarding cannabis legislation, events, activities, initiatives and discussions.

Established in 2016, the organization currently has multiple state chapter locations throughout the country, including a Northern California chapter based in Oakland. M4MM's mission is focused on providing advocacy, outreach, research, and training as it relates to the business, social reform, public policy and health/wellness in the cannabis industry.

I am pleased to introduce you to a powerful woman that I have been working with for some time.

She's smart, she's funny, she's down to earth, and she's real.

I want you all to understand why what she has to present is so valuable, and why I think she is such a dynamic woman. She's a Princeton University graduate, attended medical school and she is a former retail executive with an MBA. This brilliant mind has been intimately involved in running some of the largest, and most prestigious consumer brands in the country.

If you've ever bought anything from Target Corporation or Victoria's Secret, chances are you bought something from her. And that means you bought something from Dasheeda.

Despite all of her success, two years ago, she left a thriving 15 year career and a high paying job to become a full time cannapreneur.

Dasheeda has built her business from the ground up and employs over 10 people including her 3 sisters.

This is what we mean when we talk about creating generational wealth and keeping it all in the family.

Dasheeda is someone who understands the ins and outs of what it takes to enter this market legally, effectively and profitably. Because of that skill set, she has attracted over 20,000 followers. All of them want to understand her expertise, as it relates to cannabis, and profit from it.

What I like most about Dasheeda is her frankness, which is matched only by her compassion, and her passion for cannabis and ensuring equity for all, particularly people from communities devastated by America's drug war.

She's at the forefront of the cannabis market. We are incredibly fortunate to have her insights on making the kind of money "the wealthy" are generating with all of their privilege.

INTRODUCTION: How to Use this Workbook

If you ask 1,000 people to complete the sentence: "*I wish I had more _____.*" Ninety-four percent will say one of two things.

> The most common response is time.
>
> The second most common response?
>
> Well, that's something we'll get to in just a moment.

But first, when it comes to time, if your life is anything like mine, between work, family and the ever evolving business landscape, there are times when it feels like there just aren't enough hours in the day.

As a mother and CEO (because my time is so limited) I'm increasingly picky about which business books I read. I suspect you might be particular about what you read as well. At the same time, I know that all it takes is just one pivotal idea for a book or resource to change my life forever.

I believe this is one of those resources truly worth the investment of your time.

And not only that...

When you apply what you're about to discover, the contents and exercises in this workbook can deliver the *second* most common thing people say when asked to complete the "I wish I had more _____" sentence.

> That thing?
>
> *Money*

The reason I say that is because, as you probably already know, legalization has literally created a $10 billion industry and industry experts are saying that this plant could possibly disrupt another $500 billion worth of market applications over the next ten years.

In addition to the financial impact that legalization is creating, there are also the health and social justice aspects that are just as important. And most importantly, by the time you're finished reading and completing the exercises within this workbook, you will see how YOU can fit in and take advantage of the Green Rush. But before we dive in, because I want you to get the most out of this workbook in the least amount of time, let me explain how I would go through this workbook.

The workbook is organized as a "methodology" tool, which goes through the various roles and opportunities within the Green Rush in step-by-step detail. This workbook is intentionally designed to be *interactive*.

What I mean by that is, by necessity, there is a blurring of offline and online worlds today. The days of a written book (or even an ebook) being nothing but a "book" are long gone. More often than not, *concepts* are timeless, but with rapid changes in technology, the *application* of those concepts can change rapidly.

It is my goal to help you understand the timeless concepts and strategies and give you access to the most *up-to-date* application of those concepts at the same time. For this reason, throughout the book and at the end, we have included additional resources designed to keep you up to date with what's going on in the industry.

That said, I also want to make another super important point. I want you to understand that, in relation to the Green Rush, I've held nothing back. It is all here for you to use and customize to your personal needs. I've given you everything I can in the confines of one book for someone to understand and find their place within the Green Rush.

So there you have it. The choice is yours. Just remember, the important thing is to *start*. My team and I are committed to helping you understand the Green Rush and to give you everything you need and *more* to get you into the Green Rush.

So without further delay, let's get started!

- Dasheeda Dawson

> ## "There is room for Everybody in the new Cannabis Industry"
>
> # Invest Your Time
> ### Time > Money

The purpose of this workbook is to teach you how to leverage and invest your most valuable asset, your time, into the cannabis industry.

One of the best things about the emerging cannabis industry is that we are starting from scratch. This is the beginning, and there is room for everyone regardless of skill set or experience. No matter your passion, you can deploy it here and build a side hustle, or an empire, depending on your goals.

This book will walk you step by step through the industry, highlighting the opportunities, the segments and roles to help you find your place in this space.

I'm going to begin by sharing my story and how I became involved in the green rush, but first, let's talk about you.

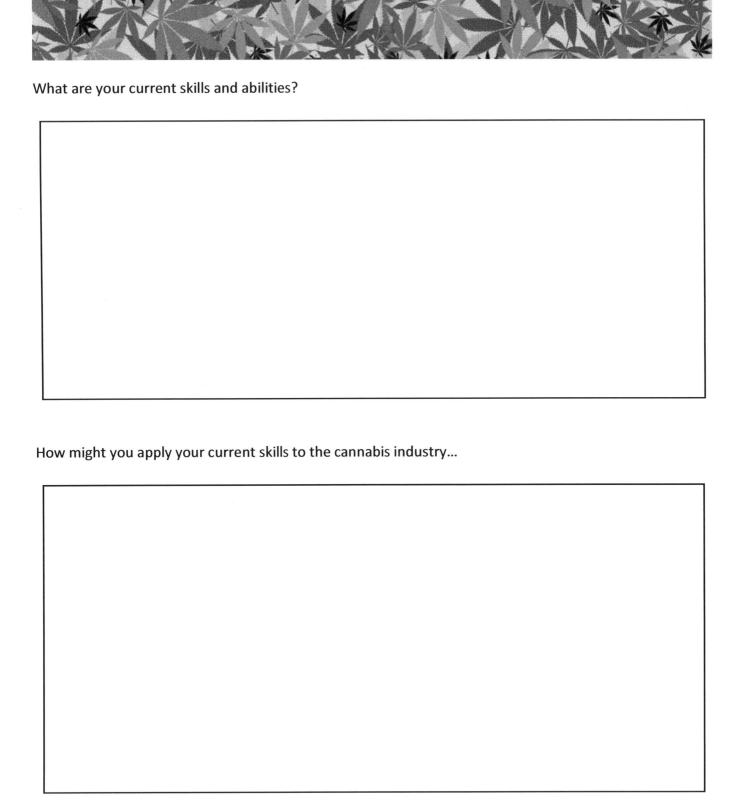

What are your current skills and abilities?

How might you apply your current skills to the cannabis industry...

MY STORY: ENTERING THIS INDUSTRY

Corporate to Cannabis Crossover

I was climbing the corporate ladder, and doing everything one would typically do to ensure a successful corporate career.

Then, I suffered a catastrophic blow. My mom passed away unexpectedly. Grief led me to question everything about my life, and ultimately walk away from my flourishing career and move west to Arizona, a medical marijuana state. Like so many people of color that I've encountered, becoming a patient was transformative for me.

So many of us have grown up under siege. I'm from East New York, a tough Brooklyn, NY neighborhood. It's not the 'new' Brooklyn that has become world renowned for artists, hipsters and craft beer. It was, and remains, hardcore. I grew up during the height of America's war on drugs. I swore off all illegal substances as a child, including cannabis. Instead, with the support of my family, I followed a very straight and narrow path: studying hard, excelling at sports, going to prep school, and then to Princeton. I was a

basketball player, so I approached life in a very strategic and disciplined way. I stayed as far away from illicit activity as I could.

Against this very Spartan existence, my mom consumed cannabis all my life. She and her friends smoked regularly. But; for me, there was a complete disconnect from their behavior, the bleak picture of drug addicts, degenerates denounced by Nancy Reagan, and the "Just Say No campaign." My sisters and I always knew that mom indulged. We just never talked about it. It just didn't seem like a big deal or a cardinal sin. I guess in the back of our minds, we realized bad people, or criminals, weren't the only ones consuming, even if we couldn't articulate it.

Fast forward a few decades. After college and three years of medical school, I decided that commerce was my calling. I attended business school and wound up in Minneapolis working as a Target Corporation executive. Around the same time, my mother was diagnosed with breast cancer. She moved in with me to seek treatment at the Mayo clinic, renowned for its world class medical facilities. Despite the amazing care she received, my mother suffered through chemo and needed cannabis for comfort. She couldn't eat, she couldn't sleep, she wasn't herself, and more than anything else; she was anxious about dying. Mom had chronic ailments on top of the cancer that left her in unbearable pain, arthritis, inflammation, and intestinal issues. Chemo aggravated and inflamed them. Only cannabis helped treat her pain.

Meanwhile, the icy cold Minnesota winter triggered my own chronic inflammation. Years of playing basketball caught up with me, leaving me with arthritis in my joints. I'd wake up feeling like a tin woman, needing time just to get moving. I was under the age of 35, but felt about eighty inside.

After watching me struggle with pain and stiffness, one day Mom invited me to smoke with her.

I resisted, but she persisted, saying "Oh child, come smoke a joint with your Mama" in a – you only live once kind of way. So I sat down and consumed cannabis for the first time.

The next day, I felt so much better!

At first, I didn't know what to make of it. Even with a molecular biology degree and medical school education, I couldn't understand how cannabis, a schedule 1 drug, could be at all beneficial. I marveled at the impact of my first joint.

All of my body's joints felt less painful and inflamed.

I'm typically an insomniac, because my brain is always on. Unless I force myself to sleep, I can stay up all night.

I actually slept through the night.

I quickly learned that this plant actually has therapeutic medicinal properties that are not yet fully understood.

But, getting my cannabis came at a cost. First and foremost, buying from the underground market for me meant a different product every time.

I didn't really know what I was getting when I got it.

I started to quietly experiment on myself, and realized almost immediately that cannabis doesn't change my ability to function. I still went to work every day and I actually start killing it. I literally became the Olivia Pope of Target Corporation, with the ability to tackle and turn around failing business units.

I came to work with less anxiety, and probably less stress than most managers, most likely because I was utilizing cannabis.

But, I would not have chosen to leave my job, or the comfortable life I had built, to come out of the cannabis closet. It took a life changing event for that to happen. After moving back to New York to lead teams at Victoria's Secret and another major Fortune 500 Company, my life was upended.

My mom was seemingly in remission, and then out of nowhere she passed away. Mom literally went to the doctor for a routine check up on a Monday, and by Friday she was gone. It was the type of tragedy that happened so fast that it shakes a person to the core. I felt like I had to disappear.

I took three weeks off from work. The first day when I returned back, I realized I had to resign. It was time for me to go because, I felt an urgency of purpose. My mom was gone, and I never really knew my father, so I felt like an orphan. After helping pay for my mother's funeral expenses and settling her estate, I knew I had to generate enough wealth to last for generations; for myself, my son and for his children.

Looking back at my career at Target Corporation, I helped the company earn what I would conservatively estimate as a half billion dollars in revenue, through my strategies and tactical leadership. But, I really hadn't even seen a fraction of 1% of that. I abandoned the corporate life, at first to heal and cope with my grief. I moved to Arizona and entered the medical marijuana community through the patient side.

Immediately, I reaped more benefits than I could imagine. I was suffering from PTSD as a result of growing up in East New York, chronic inflammation throughout my body, unknown autoimmune issues that behave like lupus, though I haven't been formally diagnosed. Issues that I'm sure a lot of other people of color have to deal with as well.

In truth, my experience entering the industry as a patient was challenging starting from the process of obtaining my medical marijuana card. The long wait times to see a medical professional and unclear payment processes could have easily deterred the average person. Then, once I walked into my first dispensary, while I was pleased to freely ask questions and select different strains, I had an extremely poor consumer experience as a patient with real ailments and as a shopper with real questions about "brands".

As a consumer marketing expert, I felt compelled to help. I knew my skills could help rebrand the industry and remove the stigma associated with being a patient. You can be highly functional and utilize cannabis all day long.

Once I entered the industry, and began traveling to legal states like Colorado, California, Oregon and Washington, too often, I was the only Black person in the boardroom. I knew I needed to share my story with other people of color. There are young brothers and sisters back home in Brooklyn, NY that are still being targeted and arrested for marijuana possession despite a decriminalization law on the books for over forty years, which disturbs me. It became clear to me that as the industry evolves, we need to be

more present as entrepreneurs and investors. As the saying goes, "If you don't have a seat at the table, you're probably on the menu."

I've now been in the business for nearly three years. I am the founder and CEO of MJM Strategy, the cannabis industry's first minority-led, digital-focused strategy and management consulting firm. MJM Strategy works on branding, strategic marketing, supply chain operations and finance, depending on our client needs.

Who is this for?
- Entrepreneurs
- Contractors / Consultants
- Professionals

This book is for anyone interested in the growing cannabis industry, from entrepreneurs thinking about entering the field, to private investors. In fact, all professions are welcome: contractors, doctors, lawyers, nurses, consultants, advisors. It will take a group effort to help build this new industry.

This book will cover the basics. The different sectors of the cannabis industry, as well as strategies for breaking in as an employee or an entrepreneur. We'll delve into plant science, and even talk a bit about investing. Once you've finished this book, you'll have the information you need to enter the cannabis industry and succeed.

Welcome to the Green Rush.

Part 1
Roles in the Legal Cannabis Industry

In this section, we will dig deeper into roles within the legal cannabis industry. Like any other industry, the legal cannabis business is comprised of specific segments with distinct roles, such as growers, distributors, resellers, dispensaries and retailers. These roles ensure that the industry thrives and becomes future-proof. So, if you're interested in the business, the first question that you must ask yourself is 'what are the most critical and fastest growing positions in the industry, and what role could I possibly play?'

Cultivator/Grower
Start growing your own cannabis

The first and most obvious position, is becoming a plant-touching entrepreneur or a grower. This is one of the industry's most important functions, since growers cultivate the plants and produce them for further downstream processing. Almost always, this is the role everyone thinks about when referencing the industry, and while it might seem like it offers the highest returns, that is not always the case. Growing is expensive, and profits aren't guaranteed. It is without question, however, the riskiest position in our current political and economic climate.

If you are interested in becoming an entrepreneur, I recommend that you start out with one of the other potential roles I'm going to outline, before jumping into cultivation.

Why would entering the cannabis industry as a plant-touching entrepreneur or grower be the riskiest proposition?

Using your skills, how can you enter the cannabis industry without handling the actual plant?

What is your why? Do you have a clear direction for what you want to accomplish by starting your business? What role could you play in the growing cannabis industry? i.e. distribution, retail, reseller

Speculators Lose Money

Let's go back through the annals of history. During the 1840s and 50s, people from all over the United States and even abroad flooded into California, hoping to strike it rich. As you have probably guessed, I'm referring to the California Gold Rush, when people from all around America and even abroad came to what was then the California Republic in search of the precious metal.

Very few gold miners ACTUALLY made money during the Gold Rush, most were lucky if they recouped their expenses. Extracting gold is an extremely difficult process requiring back-breaking labor.

Outside of panning for gold, can you think of any other ways someone might have been able to profit from California's Gold Rush?

What can you learn from the Gold Rush example as you consider entering the new Green Rush? What are potential pitfalls to avoid?

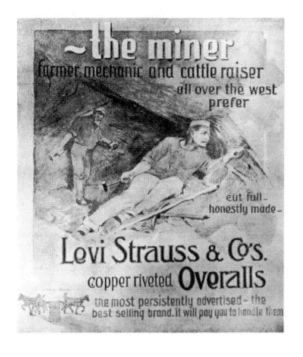

During this time, a German immigrant living in New York saw a different opportunity to strike it rich during the Gold Rush. Instead of searching for gold, he decided to sell basic goods to the gold miners. This was, for him, a much safer way to make a profit. This clever entrepreneur realized that miners needed equipment and goods, to search for gold they hoped would make them rich.

Eventually, the immigrant's most profitable product became a new style of durable pants that withstood the extreme conditions facing the gold miners. This classic "Picks and Shovels" method was created by none other than blue jeans pioneer Levi Strauss. His rugged pants were such a success, that they remain one of the world's most common articles of clothing. Today, jeans are worn by almost everyone. Some antique pairs of jeans have even become highly prized collector's items.

We are in the midst of another transformational gold rush, but this time, it's a "Green Rush" into the legal cannabis market.

Now that you've read the story of Levi Strauss, can you list 3 additional "Picks-and-Shovels" profit opportunities in the Gold Rush?

Opportunity 1

Opportunity 2

Opportunity 3

> Success is about seeing **OPPORTUNITY** where others don't...
>
> The future belongs to people who see possibilities before they become obvious.

I believe the most exciting (and profitable) companies in the cannabis industry, will be those that service the plant touching operations. They are and will continue making millions, the same way smart folks did during the Gold Rush. This is because growers and producers need materials like soil, lights, growing and hydroponic equipment, ventilation systems and services like packaging, quality control, grading and transportation.

With this "Picks and Shovels" method, companies can avoid the risks growers and producers face such as bad crops, legal regulations and pricing. In fact, there is another unreported reason why the legal marijuana market is going to grow much bigger and faster than anyone predicts: Illegal marijuana growers are also feeding the legal marijuana market!

Check the statistics. Last year, California's marijuana market was valued at $2.76 billion. But, it grew over $23 billion worth of marijuana. The remaining $20 billion came from the underground: the illegal growing, selling and usage of marijuana. Here's the thing, even illegal cannabis growers still need to buy soil, lighting, ventilation systems etc, which gives ancillary service providers access to extra billions in the market. (Please note: these numbers will likely shift as a result of California's status as an adult-use market, effective January 1, 2018.)

Can you provide 3 other ancillary products or services that cannabis growers (legal or illegal) would need to purchase to run their businesses?

Ancillary "Picks and Shovels" Opportunity #1

Ancillary "Picks and Shovels" Opportunity #2

Ancillary "Picks and Shovels" Opportunity #3

Contractor or Consultant
apply your talent to the cannabis industry

Individuals can profit from the "Picks and Shovels" approach in the cannabis industry by being consultants and applying existing skills to the bold new marketplace. For example, when marijuana becomes legal in a state, naturally more people find themselves with the freedom and the desire to grow the plant, but with limited information and resources.

So, they turn to the experts. As a result, cultivation classes are taught and reference books purchased. Growing rooms are built with complete infrastructure including electricity, adequate water supply and professional space planning. This means contractors, builders, electricians and plumbers have found a new niche where they can use their skills to build growing rooms. There are now even professional greenhouse and growing room builders in the market.

This is also a good way to enter the market if you have a complimentary skill set. It also allows you to test your abilities and experience against the market, and establish a permanent foothold in a growing industry.

In the next section, industry opportunities and areas of growth will be explored in greater detail. You'll be able to see exactly where the jobs and markets are, and how you can be competitive.

List out 3 skills that you have and how that might be applied in a "Picks and Shovels" methodology into the cannabis industry.

Skill Set & Application #1

Skill Set & Application #2

Skill Set & Application #3

TOP ROLES?

- Grow Room Construction
- Greenhouse Construction
- Security Design and Installation
- Interior Design
- IT/SEO
- Software Development
- Social Marketing
- Event Planning
- Electrical
- Product Development
- Manufacturing
- Plumbing
- Carpentry
- Professional Services

If you want to follow the "Picks and Shovels" approach, there are a variety of sectors in which to place yourself and your suitable skills and talents. As you can see from the above examples, opportunities abound across disciplines. From carpentry to social media marketing, the skills needed to fully develop this industry are immense. Whatever you do, you can find a place in this growing industry.

One of my favorite examples involves a key executive of trailblazing dispensary Harborside Health Center, which gained fame after being featured in Discovery Channel's "Weed Wars" in 2011. Yoli Felix, Harborside's creative director, is an interior designer by trade. She had no previous background in cannabis; but used her years of experience to design beautiful dispensary spaces. Her story is a perfect example of how someone can take their skills and talents from elsewhere and apply it successfully in the cannabis industry.

Attorneys can also establish lucrative niches in cannabis. Some of the industry's biggest success stories come from attorneys who started working with cannabis clients and then leveraged their newly acquired knowledge to specialize in the cannabis industry.

Pick out 3 of the roles listed above and write out how they are applicable in a "Picks and Shovels" methodology for the cannabis industry.

Role & Application #1

Role & Application #2

Role & Application #3

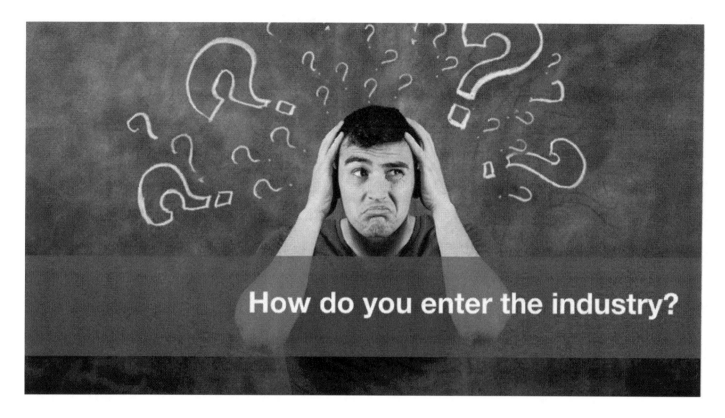

There is a lot of excitement about the cannabis industry right now. But exactly how do you open that door? How do you walk through it?

Now that you have ideas about your potential "picks and shovels" opportunities, list your top three, along with ways each will resolve a current problem for the cannabis industry.

Idea #1

Idea #2

Idea #3

Customize to this Industry

- Cannabis is different! Standard techniques often don't work.

- Take sufficient time to understand what's unique

- Identify and fill the special needs of the cannabis industry

Anyone looking to enter the cannabis industry must be aware that this is unlike other fields. Standard rules don't yet apply. Because it isn't as established as say, banking or hospitality, it's critical that prospective entrepreneurs and employees be proactive and focused on solutions. They must take the time to examine their unique skill sets and figure out how to adapt them to the industry.

The key here is looking at problems facing the industry and providing the solutions for them. This is an often overlooked classic business principle. Before you dive into cannabis you need to ask yourself, 'What are the challenges? What are the problems they have that I can solve?' and 'How do I find a unique place within this industry so that I can really carve out something special for myself?'

What special skills or know-how can you use with your "picks and shovels" idea to gain entry into the industry?

What can you do to make your offering unique?

What are some of the needs that you can satisfy in the cannabis space with your offering?

Educate yourself first

- Read
- Attend Events
- Join associations
- Work for existing cannabis company

Educating yourself is the first step. One of the mistakes many people make when trying to come into the cannabis space is not spending enough time getting educated about the industry itself. This is probably from the fear of missing out (FOMO). Cannabis is touted as the next big thing and many are rushing to carve out a place, but wind up shooting in the dark.

Entrepreneurs should have a working knowledge of the industry and a solid business plan before jumping in. It's not going anywhere, and eager entrants won't lose out by taking the time to familiarize themselves with the plant, players, products, and processes behind the burgeoning sector, so that they find their place with minimal obstacles.

Learn as much as you can about cannabis and the industry. Reading "The Pot Book," edited by Julie Holland, M.D. is a good starting point.

There are also multiple cannabis conferences and expos held across the country with different themes and orientations. Attend as many as you can. Even smaller conferences will offer valuable information and connections.

I also recommend joining associations like Minorities for Medical Marijuana and your local state or networking organizations, such as Women Grow, or Cannagather in the NY/NJ Metro region, because these are great places to have direct contact with other budding entrepreneurs in the industry. The people on the ground will be your most valuable source of real time knowledge and insight about the industry, which is still very confined to local state markets. You get to ask them real questions and get real answers from real people.

Last but not least, consider working or volunteering for an established company or advocacy organization. There is no better way than learning on the job, and many start-ups and emerging businesses will welcome the assistance.

How can you become an advocate for the cannabis industry in your area of expertise?

What are the key industry-related organizations in your area that you can volunteer for, to gain experience?

List some local start up organizations that you can reach out to, for assisting with daily tasks, shadowing opportunities and possibly offering your services pro bono or at a discounted rate.

Part 2
Sectors In The Cannabis Industry
Discover the niches in the cannabis industry so you can pick yours

In Part 2, I'm going to cover the sectors in the cannabis industry and the area's most in demand. Here, we'll take a look at specific niches, study examples of successful companies within those sectors, and review the areas with the greatest opportunities.

Genetics

- Seed
- Clones
- Tissue Culture

While I feel strongly that people should focus on ancillary businesses that don't directly involve touching the plant, any discussion of the industry must begin with cannabis itself. Plants are at the very core of this industry. Genetics play a vital role. Cannabis plant cultivation generally involves seeds and clones cut from mother plants.

Right now, tissue culture is a popular method of cultivation, as it allows producers to manufacture more clones at a lower price in a shorter period of time. This is important due to the chemical complexity of the plant.

There are a variety of different strains and each strain has unique cannabinoid and terpene profiles. This means that a deep understanding and knowledge of genetics are skills in demand offering huge dividends for those with the requisite capabilities. For example, one of the most popular strains in California is called "Tangie," bred by Crockett Family Farms. Demand is huge and has turned proprietor Dave Crockett into an enormously successful grower.

Seed Examples

In Europe, seed companies are the biggest players in the industry because the production and marketing of seeds is legal. There are virtually no major dispensaries on the continent, so most cannabis is grown and sold by individuals or small scale establishments.

Founded in 1985, Sensi Seeds is one of the most successful cannabis-related companies in the world. It is a Dutch company based in Amsterdam that markets cannabis seeds and other cannabis-related merchandise. It is the oldest and largest hemp seed producer with the world's largest hemp seed bank.

Clone Examples:

When it comes to clones, the biggest success story is Oakland California's Dark Heart nursery. When cannabis clones were first marketed, they were very fragile specimens that stood only 1.5 to 4 inches tall. Nowadays, clones produced by this company are strong and vigorous specimens that regularly stand close to a foot tall.

Tissue Culture Examples:

Because the cultivation of plants via clones and seeds is critically important in this industry, it is essential that it be done right.

Cannabis genetics have been studied for decades. The wealth of great genetic material and knowledge produced means that apprenticing under a master cannabis geneticist like Reggie Gaudino, Chief Scientific Officer at Steep Hill Labs, would provide an incredible opportunity to learn about the latest innovations in the field as they evolve. Things were very different 30 years ago. Back then, if you wanted to be a cannabis geneticist, you had to figure it out on your own.

Entering the field takes a background in science, preferably biology and an understanding of genetics. A degree is preferred, not essential. What's important is a passion for cultivation, breeding and understanding the plant.

Have a passion for biology or life sciences? In what ways can you bring your passion and know-how to the genetics segment of the cannabis industry?

In reference to seeds, what can you offer to the industry? Do you have a distinct strain to bring to market? Is it rare or unique? Is there a shortage in certain markets?

What techniques and capabilities can you bring to the cultivation aspect? Can you offer ways to improve sustainability and reduce waste?

Cultivation

- Nursery
- Sun Grown
- Light Deprivation
- Indoor
- Organic

Once the genetics are selected, planting is the next step. There are multiple methods of cultivation, which yield cannabis with different properties and characteristics. Commercial cultivation usually occurs in a nursery.

There are 3 main ways of growing cannabis:

1. **Outdoor Growing**: Where the plants are grown in an open field with plenty of natural sunlight. How cannabis has been cultivated for thousands of years.
2. **Greenhouse Growing**: Plants are grown in greenhouses where cultivators can manipulate the light cycle to get higher quality yield than growing outdoors.
3. **Indoor Growing**: Similar to greenhouse growing, cultivators get higher quality yields by exerting more control over the growth cycle than the outdoor method. However, indoor growing uses high-intensity lamps that require a large amount of electricity, which may increase the overall carbon footprint.

Nursery

- Growing live plants for other growers
- Growing live plants for retail sales

A nursery is an ideal place to grow cannabis. Currently, the number of cultivators and grow operations using nurseries is increasing exponentially. Just a few years ago, growers would have to produce their own clones in small rooms, almost always with inadequate equipment and resources. Those clones required time, space and significant financial investment.

Today the process has become more streamlined. Because clones and tissue cultures are readily available, growers of all sizes can cultivate good, clean and healthy cannabis. Generally, nurseries grow the plants from clones and tissue cultures and sell them wholesale to cultivators. This is an opportunity for savvy entrepreneurs to grow and sell plants.

Is growing cannabis a realistic option for you? Are you in a legalized state? If so, what are the requirements for a cultivation license? If you grow, will you sell your product to cultivators or wholesalers?

[ ]

If you are not in a legal state, what are some unique ways to enter this sector? How can you utilize the digital space?

[ ]

Can you provide tools to aid the growing process?

[ ]

Sun Grown Examples:

As the cannabis industry grows, so does the market for the sun-grown pesticide free variety. There are now brands that specialize in this kind of cannabis. Brands like Swami Select created by California based guru Swami Chaitanya. Chaitanya, called the "the Swami of Pot" by *Rolling Stone* magazine, is also considered a holy man who uses cannabis as inspiration.

Before the legalization, his picture didn't appear on the packaging, likely to reduce the possibility of arrest and prosecution. However, first as private growers, then as purveyors of Swami Select, he and partner Nikki Lastreto have been in this business for decades promoting craft cannabis.

Marigold California is another highly respected craft cannabis brand. Renowned for its quality, Marigold is a cultivator collective dedicated to growing quality cannabis with a low carbon impact. Also prominent in the craft cannabis movement is Ganja Rebel Seeds, a company that produces high quality seeds innovating cannabis genetics in the process.

The name "Ganja Rebel Seeds" itself is steeped in meaning, as it represents the advocates' fight for legalization and respect. In the words of the company's elusive founder, "There were people who did everything they possibly could to stop us. There are people who sacrificed their lives to bring us to where we are. We had to be rebels and that's part of our heritage, and we should hold it close to us and never let it go".

Lamp Grown
Growing plants for Flower

Lamp grown cannabis represents another type of popular plant production. Cannabis grown indoors with artificial lighting still dominates the market, despite the high carbon footprint. The advantage of growing cannabis indoors is undeniable. The results are high quality cannabis flower, often referred to as "jewels". A rapidly growing trend has been the use of LED lights in the cannabis industry to help improve energy efficiency without sacrificing quality indoor cultivation.

Lamp Grown Examples:

- Dr. Greenthumb
- LiveWell
- DragonFish

High Latitude Farms founded by two career mariners in Hood River, Oregon is a leading indoor hydroponically grown cannabis brand which has grown rapidly by leveraging the power of social media.

Canada, our neighbors to the north, is now one of just two countries where cannabis is fully legal. Canadian based LiveWell Foods is one of the largest indoor-grown cannabis companies in the country, with more than 1.5 million square feet of cultivation facilities and a world-class research and innovation centre. The company's stock is publicly traded on the Canadian Securities Exchange. Dragon Fish, a Californian brand, specializes in growing hard to cultivate strains of cannabis. Their most famous product is called Red Congolese, an intense strain of cannabis. Each of these three brands has their own niches even within the indoor-grown cannabis sector. Dr. Greenthumb is a luxury brand with high-end and high-priced products. LiveWell is more focused on advanced scientific research to deliver prescription and consumer health products for the masses, while Dragon Fish specializes in rare hard-to-grow strains.

Organic

In the United States, cannabis currently can't technically be called 'organic,' because it is still considered illegal under US federal law. Organic standards are determined by specific requirements that must be verified by USDA, an impossibility given the designation of cannabis as a schedule 1 drug. Growers risk, among other challenges, fines of up to $11,000 levied by the US Department of Agriculture for improper labelling. An alternate naturally-grown certification makes sense, particularly when it comes to the health and wellness benefits of the plant.

Harborside Health Center partnered with Chris Van Hook, an organic certifier for farms to adapt the protocols, techniques and procedures for the cannabis industry and create a cannabis related certification called "Clean Green". Other associations like Americans for Safe Access and the California Growers Association also have their own versions of organic certifications.

Becoming a cultivator in the legal cannabis industry means becoming licensed, one of the most difficult steps to doing business in this rapidly evolving space. In most states, licensing is a complex and expensive endeavor and should be navigated with the help of project management consultants, which can tip total costs into the million dollar range. People with the passion and desire to grow, but not millions in disposable income should focus on learning the skills of cannabis cultivation with the goal of getting work at established grow operation, or look to relocate to a state like Oregon or Oklahoma, where the costs of entering the market are relatively low.

If you are looking to enter into the cultivation field, what organizations in your area can help you with the process? Is there an M4MM chapter in your area?

How will your plants be different from the others in this segment? Are your seeds different? Is your plant grown in a greenhouse? Is your plant grown outdoors with natural sunlight?

What practices can you use to have your plant stand out? Will you use organic soil? What about hydroponics?

Processing & Extraction

- Equipment
- CO_2, H_2O, BHO, SHO, Alcohol.
- R&D/Formulation
- Production

Until recently, small growers, together with teams of trimmers, did processing of cannabis right on the farm or grow site. That proved inefficient and difficult. Now, companies that handle the cannabis processing have launched. They weigh, trim and package that crop for further distribution.

Extraction is an emerging sector in the cannabis industry with tremendous growth potential. Extraction is the process of removing the plant's active ingredients and concentrating them, converting them into a form that's usable for the consumer. One method uses carbon dioxide. Another, involving only ice and water, has been used for thousands of years. The mixture is agitated and strained to collect very potent concentrations of hashish, the concentrated resin from cannabis.

One of the most popular methods of extraction today involves butane, hexane or other types of heavy industrial solvents. Because of concerns about carcinogens and unknown side effects, usage of heavy solvents have slowed considerably and are actively being phased out of the industry. Alternatively, solvent free extracts involving only heat and pressure to extract are considered more natural and mild. Alcohol

extraction is also an option, and very popular among cancer patients who use Rick Simpson oil, which is credited for reducing the growth of tumors and cancer cells.

Recently, sophisticated laboratories using different types of extraction formulas have emerged. These labs provide contract services to companies that manufacture and distribute vape cartridges. Working with these labs gives concentrate companies a competitive edge because of the higher quality and more consistent products generated. Production is growing rapidly and if you're interested, be sure to read up on traditional and modern forms of extraction as well as the latest trends. Entry into the space involves getting licensed, and can be complicated and expensive. Different states have different extraction laws and regulations. Pick a place to set up operations with access to high quality and inexpensive cannabis and a robust legal market.

It's an investment, but for individuals with drive and capital can be quite lucrative. Three years ago vaporizer pen sales amounted to only low single digits of overall cannabis product sales, and right now their market share amounts to almost 30 percent and climbing. In terms of future growth opportunities, you want to follow the market into concentrates and infused products.

Does your skill include production? What legal state can you set up shop in? How can you tailor the process uniquely to your set of skills?

Do you have an idea that will make production in the industry run smoother, or make the process better?

What can you think of that is missing in the production sector or what do you think you can provide?

Extraction Examples:

- Moxie
- Blue River Terps
- Loud Pack/Green Wolf
- Gold Drops

Right now, there are a plethora of cannabis products in virtually every market, from beverages to edibles, with more introduced every day. Many of them are made with cannabis extracts, each with its own flavor derived from terpene and cannabinoid profiles. As previously mentioned, the extraction sector is the fastest growing of all the plant touching categories, and here are a few companies innovating in the space.

Moxie, a cannabis extract company founded in 2015, is a leader in the concentrate space. The company utilizes laboratory testing and strict safety standards to ensure the quality of its products. Other concentrate brands like Blue River Terpenes combine full spectrum terpenes and the latest solventless technologies to guarantee better ingredients and better product experiences.

Producing shatter, wax, budder, snap and pull oil

Once extraction is complete, the resulting substance is converted into another usable form. Cannabis oils can be difficult to transport and use. Extraction companies convert the oils into wax, shatter, budder, snap and pull, drier and easier-to-handle formats.

Extractions satisfy the need for a concentrated and more potent cannabis experience. Oils were probably the first extractions, and innovation has created the room to explore new textures and formats.

Live resin is one such novel format. In order to create live resin, versus traditional resins like hashish, fresh cannabis flowers are used, rather than dried plant material. The technique produces an extract richer in terpenes. If creating concentrates piques your interest, make the necessary investment to learn the myriad techniques. Take a class to learn how to make concentrates or the latest innovation in extraction technology. You can become an apprentice under a hash maker to learn age-old methods. For example, The Dank Duchess is one of the only African-American hashmakers in the world and she received her education from direct hands-on experience with legendary hashish artist, Frenchy Cannoli. Immerse yourself fully, whether your goal is to found a multinational conglomerate or work at a concentrate company.

What steps can you take to get into the extraction sector of the industry? Name three steps you can take right now.

Step #1

Step #2

Step #3

Formulation

The science of putting together cannabinoids and other active chemicals to achieve a distinct result on efficacy.

Scientific discovery and innovation in the cannabis industry have led to a robust formulation subcategory. Cannabis is made up of between 65 to 400 unique chemical compounds. Each has specific effects on the human body and mind. Formulation is essentially the art of identifying these different compounds and expressing them to achieve optimal results.

People who've worked with the plant have always understood that different strains of cannabis have varying effects on the human body, but initially didn't know why, and certainly didn't understand how to fully manipulate those effects.

The advent of specialized analytical equipment to test cannabis, and the ability to do it relatively cheaply and quickly helps the industry understand both the different compound profiles of each strain and ways to manipulate the profile to fulfill consumer's specific needs.

Do you have skills and interest necessary to explore formulation? How can you enter the sector? What would your process be?

What can you formulate to make a distinct product in this sector?

How can you better the process? Can you change the process to produce a unique product?

Formulation Innovation

- **Therapeutic:** Prana, Aunt Zelda's
- **User experience:** Ebbu
- **Onset:** 1906
- **Efficiency:** Vipova Tea

Cannabis formulation is led by research driven innovation. Companies like Prana and Aunt Zelda's produce plant based medicines with distinct cannabinoid profiles targeting different medical conditions. Companies like Ebbu, which is editing the cannabis genome, are examining and restructuring the plant on a cellular level using modern technology.

And, 1906, which developed a rapid activation edible using a technique to significantly reduce onset time of cannabis. Generally, it takes about 45 minutes for a user to feel the effects after ingesting a cannabis-infused product. 1906 boasts products with an onset time of 20 minutes or less.

Vipova Tea credits its patented DehydraTECH ™ technology for the enhanced bioavailability of its CBD infused tea, allowing the company to use less CBD in their products, and still maintain a positive effect on the human body.

These companies are on the cutting edge of cannatech, and innovative entrepreneurs interested in this space should read up on the latest infusion technology and figure how it can be applied in the cannabis space. They can also leverage age-old methods to formulate more traditional products such as tinctures, sublingual sprays, syrups, and topicals that have been used for centuries.

Delivery Mechanisms
- Vaporizors
- Pens/cartridges
- Patches
- Buccal lozenges
- Suppositories

Delivery mechanisms are experiencing explosive growth as consumption methods have become far more sophisticated than just smoking a joint. This sector specializes in devices that can be used to consume cannabis. There have been a number of notable breakthroughs in the past ten years.

In this category, vaporizers, which gently heat cannabis to release activated THC without burning, have arguably had the greatest impact. Vaping virtually eliminates the risk of creating carcinogenic smoke while consuming cannabis. In the past, vaporizers were bulky, expensive and difficult to use. While much more streamlined, today's high end vapes can cost more than a thousand dollars. Those price points made them out of reach for average consumers, until the entry of more reasonable priced models into the market.

Vape pens, which can now be purchased for less than $20, have become immensely popular as they allow people to use cannabis easily and discreetly, without the discomfort of smoking. The traditional method requires consumers to grind their weed, roll it into a joint, and light it, creating smoke, odor and ash. However, vaporizer technology continues to evolve and there is still room for improvement.

Skin patches are another amazing new format for cannabis delivery. Mary's Medicinals transdermal skin patches are industry leaders, dispensing cannabis through the veins and providing 8-12 hours of relief with CBD or THC.

Buccal lozenges are another emerging form of cannabis delivery. They are little lozenges placed between the cheek and the teeth that gradually melt into the gum tissue. It bypasses the digestive system, and unlike typical edibles or gummies, users start feeling the effects in about 10 minutes.

Finally, there are suppositories. This may come as a surprise, but suppositories are the single most efficient way of taking in cannabis. If users can overcome the discomfort, they offer the biggest bang for the buck.

Could you enter the delivery mechanism sector? What could you bring to this area with your expertise?

Vape pens have become increasingly popular. How would you innovate or improve upon this delivery format, or create an alternative?

Do you have ideas that might aid with delivery products?

Infusion

- Cannaceuticals: Prana, Auntie Zelda's
- Beverages: Dixie
- Edibles: Kiva, Bhang, Altai
- Topicals: Mary's Medicinals, Dr. Green's

There is a wide array of cannabis infusions currently on the market. These products can be classified into four main categories.

Cannaceuticals

These products look and feel like something that you get from a vitamin store; these usually come in a tincture or capsule form.

Beverages

The first cannabis-infused beverages were produced by Dixie, and were considered soft drinks. Infused teas and coffees are now available, as well as many other new beverages on the market.

Edibles

Infused foods most often come in the form of traditional confections - these are very popular. Currently, there are more sweet cannabis foods than savory healthy options on the market. The top-selling cannabis edible in the industry by far is still the cannabis brownie.

In fact, edible companies with sophisticated packaging, branding, and marketing campaigns for their products are emerging. One such example is Kiva, which produces award-winning chocolate bars from an indica-dominant hybrid strain in a range of flavors.

Topicals

These are cannabis-infused products applied directly on the skin, and they are incredibly effective.

Let me share with you a heart-warming incident I recently witnessed.

I was in a dispensary, walking past a bench where I spotted a sample jar of cannabis-infused hand lotion. I saw an older woman sitting on the bench with tears running down her cheeks. Concerned, I walked over to see what was wrong. She looked up at me, and broke into a smile, reassuring me that nothing was wrong.

She was crying tears of joy, because for the first time in eight years, she was able to unclench her hands.

Topicals provide a great low barrier to entry for people unfamiliar with wellness benefits of cannabis products. If you have a parent or relative with a backache or an inflamed knee, who is resistant to using cannabis as a treatment, try to convince them to sample a cannabis topical.

I believe there is a huge opportunity for people to keep expanding and innovating in the topicals category. Here, home remedies have been tremendously effective, and the only thing savvy entrepreneurs need are the willingness to experiment and perfect their products.

If you reviewed the history of cannabis, you would find that topical application is one of the most widespread therapeutic uses for the plant. For example in Mexico, cannabis has been soaked in rubbing alcohol and used for treating muscle and joint ailments for centuries.

Are you in the beauty industry? How can you incorporate cannabis into your products?

Do you have a food or a beverage that you can infuse with cannabis? How can you make this stand out?

Can you create infused varieties that you can package and sell to others?

Veterinary
- Prevention
- Pain relief
- Cancer

Every living creature on the planet (with the exception of insects) has an endocannabinoid system. This includes the pets we have at home.

A number of veterinary health issues respond incredibly well to cannabis. In fact, cannabis-infused veterinary products are turning up increasingly on dispensary shelves, including options like medicated doggy treats and pet-specific tinctures.

Do you have an idea of services that can improve the veterinary field?

What are some products in animal health that would benefit from cannabis?

Are there some techniques that are used in treating animals that you can improve on using cannabis?

Packaging

- Flowers
- Extracts
- Food & Beverages
- Seeds & Clones

Packaging is yet another area with a huge amount of potential, and as an ancillary or non-plant touching business, doesn't face the same level of federal scrutiny as other businesses.

Growing up, cannabis packaging meant ziplock bags (the dime bag). Packaging did not get much better when the medical cannabis industry started in California over 20 years ago.

However, step into any dispensary now, and you'll see an amazing variety of beautiful packages, with emphasis on both presentation as well as functionality.

Packaging Innovation

- Eco- friendly
- Child proof
- Smell proof
- Locking
- Bulk
- Premium
- Travel

There is a whole range of white space opportunities to explore under the packaging category.

One potential niche involves coming up with packaging for individual, delicate, living cannabis clones to facilitate transportation. This is a big challenge - the transport journey can sometimes take up to 4 or 8 hours and involve difficult climatic conditions. Specialized packaging has to help the clone withstand it.

Another, involves coming up with eco-friendly packaging. The cannabis community places high value on its respect for Mother Nature. However, most cannabis packaging is neither sustainable nor eco-friendly.

Childproof packaging is also experiencing rapid growth. This is because US states and jurisdictions are now mandating that cannabis be sold in childproof packaging. Generally, the packaging is unflattering and inconspicuous. Inventing a form of childproof cannabis packaging that does not destroy the marketability of the product is the industry's equivalent of building a better mousetrap.

The distinct odor of cannabis presents another opportunity for evolution. Many people aren't comfortable with the strong smell of terpenes lingering on them as they carry their stash around - which makes it a great niche for innovation. In fact, there are a number of products developed to counter this issue, like smell-proof plastic bags, as well as women's purses and handbags equipped with smell-proof technology and childproof locks.

Cannabis must be transported in massive quantities for processing; presenting another packaging opportunity. The harvested plants are moved from grower to the extractor and from the extractor to the manufacturer. How does one put twenty five gallons of extremely viscous cannabis oil into a container, so that it can be transported and emptied in a way that ensures achieving maximum yield and little to no waste?

Silicone concentrate or extract carriers have become the go-to solution for both large-size and small scale cannabis oil packaging in recent years. Cannabis extracts are often sticky, and if you put them in glass or plastic, you will end up wasting a lot of extract because you will not be able to get it off. However, it peels right off silicone, so these silicone vials and containers for extracts have become hugely popular.

Travel friendly packaging also represents a huge opportunity. Cannabis consumer friendly laws are still relatively rare. Many cannabis patients travel between friendly and unfriendly environments, and discreet packaging could mean the difference between access and arrest. Please note that I am in no way advocating for bringing cannabis into illegal environments. Consumers do so at their own risk.

Delving into packaging requires a background in design and partnership with a qualified manufacturer, or starting your own manufacturing unit. Cost for entry can add up, so be prepared for a significant financial investment. However, the potential upside is huge.

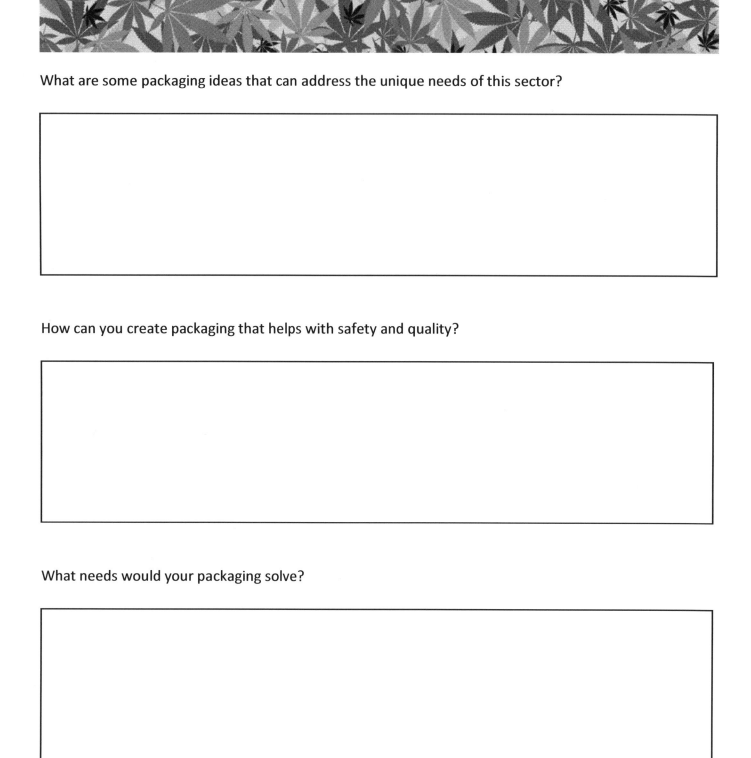

What are some packaging ideas that can address the unique needs of this sector?

How can you create packaging that helps with safety and quality?

What needs would your packaging solve?

Software or Information Technology

- POS/Inventory/Tracking
- Ordering platforms
- Social media
- Recommendation engine
- Trading platform (Tradiv, Addistry)

There is a tremendous demand for software and IT in the cannabis industry, and plenty of room for new people to get involved.

The first industry specific products here were one-size-fits-all point of sale systems like BioTrack and MJ Freeway.

Now, cannatech offerings have expanded to incorporate ordering platforms that connect consumers with dispensaries, as well as the development of social media platforms that connect cannabis aficionados, creating a social environment for them to engage. New brands such as Jade Insights and CannaTrax have emerged to provide more refined and customized business intelligence solutions.

In addition, there are content driven platforms designed to help consumers make informed cannabis related choices such as EstroHaze, Leafly and Merry Jane.

For those interested in Business-to-Business (B2B) transactions, trading platforms function almost like commodities exchanges. Companies like Americanex and Cannabis Hemp Exchange (CHEX) provide platforms where wholesalers, retailers, and growers can interact and do business. Plus, they actually provide free market commerce, a rarity in the cannabis industry, which functions very much a gray market because of the plant's designation as a schedule 1 drug.

Joining the cannatech revolution is as simple (and as complicated) as creating the next great website, app or data system to propel the industry forward. Programmers, coders, software designers, app developers and all other tech lovers welcome.

If you are in the information technology sector, what type of services could you provide?

Can you implement a technological process that helps solve some of the industry's challenges?

Can you transfer skills like human resources, IT, content creation, and compliance and carve a niche in this sector?

Like any industry, marketing is essential for cannabis businesses. Every enterprise must promote its products and services to potential consumers using advertising, promotions, public relations and sales, the core components of any strategic marketing plan, whether targeting other businesses or individual consumers. Because cannabis is for the moment, illegal on the federal level, marketing in the industry is more nuanced and proscribed than other sectors.

What are three ways you can use public relations and marketing skills to assist the cannabis industry?

Idea #1

Idea #2

Idea #3

Event Marketing

Advertising in mainstream outlets is currently very challenging and limited. Events are perhaps the most prevalent form of marketing in the cannabis industry, particularly when it comes to the B2B niche. Conferences like MJBizCon, Cannabis World Congress & Business Expo (CWCBE) and NECANN are designed to provide an industry overview, while events like IC3 are geared towards pairing investors with cannabis companies looking for capital.

There are cannabis conferences designed for almost every facet of the industry; information technology, the medical market and consumer education, including the Cannabis Education Advocacy Symposium & Expo (CEASE). CEASE is a consumer focused non-profit organization that I created to educate the public about the fact-based health and wellness benefits of the plant while highlighting the latest developments in state and federal legislation, social justice and business.

Big cannabis brands crave traditional advertising channels and a number of media outlets, both digital and print have cropped up to close the gap. Examples include High Times, one of the oldest cannabis publications, Sensi, Broccoli, which is aimed at women, and Emerald magazine.

Content Marketing Examples:

ESTROHAZE

weedmaps

Some of the most recognizable and respected brands in the content marketing niche are service oriented digital platforms such as Leafly, Weedmaps and EstroHaze, a platform dedicated to connecting people of color to the cannabis movement. Creating a content platform is a relatively low-cost way to add your voice to the cannabis industry. An understanding of SEO, content curation and a regular posting schedule are necessities for launching and growing online platforms. Magazines and other print publications involve a higher level of investment, but custom publishers can help streamline those efforts.

Content is a powerful draw because stories teach us what it means to be human. Media created for cannabis has the potential to educate millions about the powers of plant medicine, dispelling myths and over 80 years of propaganda.

There is a huge thirst for cannabis knowledge and re-education. Prohibition has led to decades of misinformation and stigma; as the legalization movement grows, so do the millions around the globe seeking the truth.

There is tremendous opportunity to introduce people to cannabis culture and enhance the knowledge of those already involved.

Influencer Marketing Examples:

Dollar for dollar, influencer marketing is one of the most effective ways to build and scale a brand online, boost consumer engagement, and raise overall awareness of a product or service. By tapping into a trendsetter's existing fan base, savvy entrepreneurs can turbocharge the growth of their businesses. The audience is built-in, the secret is establishing win-win partnership that offer value to both parties. Affiliate sales programs, paid sponsorships and promotions and in-kind donations are all ways to work with influencers to introduce brands to new audiences and generate new leads.

There is tremendous opportunity to both become cannabis influencers and to leverage existing platforms. Social media savvy individuals unafraid to openly support cannabis and share their experiences can amass thousands of followers. The key is consistency, and using hashtags on prominent channels like Facebook, Instagram and Twitter to join and create community.

Working with existing influencers involves creating strategic alliances that make sense for both parties. Offering someone with a six figure following free swag in exchange for promotion is an affront, and a waste of your time. Treat these deals as you would any celebrity endorsement, influencers are micro (and sometimes bonafide) celebrities who deserve and demand commissions, paid product placement and sponsorships.

The good news is that there are influencers at every popularity level, so find the most popular and professional that your budget will allow. The most successful influencer marketing programs work with a range of personalities with both large and small platforms. Each deal should be unique to the influencer.

What are some content or event marketing ideas to expand awareness about the industry and attract more consumers?

```
┌─────────────────────────────────────────────────────────────────────────┐
│                                                                         │
│                                                                         │
│                                                                         │
│                                                                         │
└─────────────────────────────────────────────────────────────────────────┘
```

How can you take your content creation skills and apply them to the cannabis industry?

```
┌─────────────────────────────────────────────────────────────────────────┐
│                                                                         │
│                                                                         │
│                                                                         │
│                                                                         │
└─────────────────────────────────────────────────────────────────────────┘
```

Do you have marketing experience that can help other websites and businesses in this industry? How can you best use it?

```
┌─────────────────────────────────────────────────────────────────────────┐
│                                                                         │
│                                                                         │
│                                                                         │
│                                                                         │
└─────────────────────────────────────────────────────────────────────────┘
```

Retail

- Dispensary
- Farm to Table
- Delivery
- On-site Consumption
- Subscription boxes: 420 Goodybox

Retail operations represent the front lines of the cannabis industry, selling flower and other products directly to consumers. Brick and mortar dispensaries are the most visible part of the retail sector, though there are many other novel ways to get cannabis from the grower to the consumer.

There are farm-to-table models, companies that source cannabis directly from growers and deliver straight to the consumer's home. Delivery companies also work with dispensaries, adding an additional level of convenience and customer service to retail storefronts. For people who want to choose their own products and explore them in person, there are dispensaries that offer attractive visual displays and even on-site consumption.

Subscription boxes are also a retail option growing in popularity as more users embrace cannabis. Most subscription services like Hemper and 420 Goodybox contain cannabis related accessories. I believe that soon, we'll see subscription boxes that actually contain cannabis, particularly in states that allow adult use.

Are you a delivery driver or in a field where cannabis delivery is possible? How can you participate in that business?

Do you have a retail space that you can add products that include cannabis, (note these can also be CBD products, which are non-psychotropic and subject to fewer regulations)?

What steps can you take to enter the retail space? What are some ideas that will make your store unique?

Tourism

- Tours
- Accommodation
- Services (High End Transportation, Cannabis Concierge)
- Meet Ups

Adult use legalization has created a booming market for cannabis tourism in the United States and abroad.

People from cannabis-prohibited areas are flocking to places with legal access to consume cannabis and experience the local culture. Like any other tourists, they want to sample the local scene, which includes touring dispensaries, farms and other cannabis themed destinations. They are going to want to see all facets of the local cannabis community including manufacturing as well as where and how locals consume.

There is massive potential for tourism in adult-use friendly areas. Think of it like tourism in wine countries.

Those tourists will need cannabis friendly accommodations, a stark contrast to the hotels where tourists are required to pay hefty penalties if they consume in their rooms. There is a huge opportunity here to capitalize on tourism by creating accommodations without draconian restrictions for cannabis users.

There are also vaporizer rental services available in Denver, which are ideal for visitors unwilling to spend upwards of $500 on devices that they cannot use at home.

Cannabis concierge consultants, like Tanganyika of Jayn Green who specializes in international cannabis tourism, help curate the cannabis experiences for out-of-towners and busy locals. They function as personal guides introducing tourists and guests to the area's cannabis community and culture.

While opening up cannabis friendly hotels may be prohibitively expensive for many would-be entrepreneurs, there is a place in the tourism industry for everyone. Starting a cannabis themed tour or opening up a concierge business is as simple as getting to know your local industry and its players, and creating a compelling digital presence--website, social media platforms etc. You can build a fun, exciting and profitable business based on local goods and services. When it comes to figuring out a role in the blossoming cannabis tourism industry, the only limit is your imagination.

Can you turn your passion for meeting new people into a business? What can you offer in the tourism sector?

What tools can you use to create a distinctive cannabis themed experience for others in your home state?

Do you have a space to create a one of a kind cannabis experience for cannacurious people?

Events

- Events
- Music
- Industry
- Athletic
- Culinary

- Farm to table (Flow Kana)
- Parties
- Food
- Cannabis cups

Providing education and empowerment can happen in numerous ways, such events offering people face-to-face contact with advocates, innovators and positive experiences in controlled settings.

There was a time when bringing together too many cannabis consumers in one place might trigger a police raid.

Now, there are safe spaces to celebrate cannabis culture and enjoy the incredible creativity and sense of connection that comes from the plant, and fellowship with other cannabis consumers.

Name some different types of events that you can use to promote cannabis. How would you provide attendees with an unforgettable experience?

```
┌─────────────────────────────────────────────────────────────────────┐
│                                                                     │
│                                                                     │
│                                                                     │
│                                                                     │
└─────────────────────────────────────────────────────────────────────┘
```

Do your skills involve party planning? How can you create a premium cannabis experience?

```
┌─────────────────────────────────────────────────────────────────────┐
│                                                                     │
│                                                                     │
│                                                                     │
│                                                                     │
└─────────────────────────────────────────────────────────────────────┘
```

What are some ways you can bring skills of cooking or entertainment into the cannabis industry?

```
┌─────────────────────────────────────────────────────────────────────┐
│                                                                     │
│                                                                     │
│                                                                     │
│                                                                     │
└─────────────────────────────────────────────────────────────────────┘
```

Sales & Distribution

- Processing
- Distribution
- Transport
- Wholesale

Sales and distribution is essentially the system of moving cannabis from the point of production to the other parts of the supply chain, in order to get it to the consumer.

The first step is cannabis processing.

Once the cannabis is processed and ready to be shipped, it must be moved from point A to point B. Distribution companies satisfy that need.

For decades, such activities have involved tremendous risk. Individuals distributing or transporting cannabis (drug trafficking) faced steeper penalties than small-time growers and dealers. These types of businesses existed almost exclusively on the black market. However, as cannabis legalization evolves, many companies are stepping into this necessary role; they collect the cannabis from the growers or the processors, and move it to the manufacturers or direct to the dispensaries.

Some of these distributors purchase the cannabis and resell it, while others act solely as transportation outfits charging fees for hauling the harvested plants.

This is an emerging portion of the industry that is ripe for improvement through increased competition.

Distribution Examples:
- In the shadows until very recently
- RVR
- Altai
- Calyx Brands

Distribution is relatively new everywhere and really emergent in California, the only state with a mandatory level of distributors.

Some alcohol companies who have traditionally distributed wines and spirits are getting into the business and setting up new entities. In fact, in the initial roll-out of adult-use legalization in Nevada, only alcohol distributors were awarded licenses to distribute cannabis.

Also, some of the larger cannabis manufacturers have expanded their services and are distributing the products of their competitors alongside their own. Distribution only companies are just starting to spring up. This is an attractive entry point for people in legal markets with trucking or delivery experience and relationships with local growers and processors.

Are you in sales? How can you transfer that skill to the cannabis industry?

[blank box]

As you in transportation or logistics? How could you transfer that skill into the cannabis industry?

[blank box]

What other ancillary skill or resource can you bring into the cannabis industry?

[blank box]

Real Estate

- Property acquisition (purchase + lease / purchase + flip)
- Property development
- Project financing
- Project design & management

We've covered all of the categories dealing directly with the plant, but the following ancillary markets are in some ways just as critical. Properly zoned real estate is essential for getting into any facet of the cannabis business. And, there are companies designed to help cannabis businesses identify and develop real estate.

Their services run the gamut from purchasing real estate on behalf of cannabis companies and leasing it back to developing properties to providing financing for build out and development. Not to mention architects and contracting firms with the expertise to design and manage construction.

Real estate professionals can come into the cannabis industry and specialize in any those particular areas. In fact, almost every skill set has a counterpart in cannabis.

The industry is actively seeking people in real estate and there are significant premiums for working in the space. Seasoned real estate professionals can deploy their current skills and contacts and reap significant gains.

However, entering the cannabis real estate market is not without risk.

There is speculative risk, but that is normal for all real-estate transactions. However, there is one major risk you take on in cannabis, albeit slight, and that is civil forfeiture, the federal government's right to seize any property being used for cannabis because it remains a schedule 1 drug.

The probability of a civil forfeiture is slight because of rare bipartisan support for banning the DEA from using federal forfeiture funds in its war on drugs. The current administration has also testified in front of Congress, promising not to conduct these types of seizures. However, until a ban is codified into law, the risk, though slight, remains.

Are you in finance? How can you transfer that skill to the cannabis industry?

How can you transfer real estate services to the cannabis industry? Can you lease property? Can you assist in finding property?

What other ancillary skill or resource can you bring into the cannabis industry?

Insurance
- Crop insurance
- Liability insurance
- Workman comp
- Theft and fire

As the cannabis industry matures, the need and accessibility of insurance to manage some of the related risks also grows.

This is especially true when high level investors become involved in cannabis projects. The investors want assurances that in the event of a bad crop, a worker's slip and fall judgment, or criminal activity and acts of God, that some portion of their investments can be recouped.

When the industry began, insurance companies avoided cannabis assiduously. However, as the cannabis movement gains popularity and momentum, companies willing to work with industry businesses have come forward to offer insurance for a variety of activities.

What are some insurance services that you can provide for cannabis businesses?

Can you provide consulting advice for start-up cannabis businesses in the insurance sector?

Can you create insurance plans tailored to the cannabis industry?

Human Resources
- Recruiting
- Training
- Outsourced HR
- Payroll

Human resources and management is another one of those basic services that must be provided in order for the industry to stabilize and operate like more traditional sectors such as banking or healthcare.

1. Recruiting
2. Training
3. Payroll processing
4. Employee Relations

Every company with more than one employee will need human resources support for recruiting, training, payroll and benefits, and employee relations. Companies like Wurk now provide a full suite of outsourced HR services to cannabis businesses, while others like Vangst, Hemp Staff and THC Staffing focus on recruiting. HR professionals looking to enter the industry can start businesses or look for human resources roles at established cannabis companies.

List three ways to provide unique services in the human resources sector.

Idea #1

Idea #2

Idea #3

Legal

- Real estate
- Transactional
- Regulatory
- Government relations
- Compliance
- Criminal
- IP
- Employment/labor

The cannabis industry was created and is governed by laws and countless regulations. Therefore, attorneys and compliance officers are essential to the industry's growth and success. Opportunities exist in every specialty, from real estate to regulatory law, to government relations and criminal law. The need for qualified legal professionals is almost inexhaustible. Attorneys practicing in legalized states can brush up on the current law, and in many cases jump right into the industry. As someone with experience working in partnership with legal experts, I find intellectual property protections and employment/labor law with respect to cannabis to be particularly interesting. Frankly, as long as cannabis is federally illegal, there will be a need for criminal lawyers in the industry.

How can you transfer your legal skills to the cannabis sector?

Can you create contracts to help cannabis businesses, or help broker deals between companies?

How can you get involved to advocate for legal change in the cannabis industry?

Education

- Consumers
- Entrepreneurs
- Employees
- Regulators
- Executives
- Technical
- Compliance

Though I touched on education briefly in a previous section, it is so important that I must expound. Cannabis isn't just an industry, it's a movement. Knowledge is the most critical step to ensuring that all people have access to the plant's wellness benefits. Educators and education are paramount to the industry's continued growth and development.

Consumers need education about the plant and available products, the best way to purchase them, and fair pricing.

Entrepreneurs and prospective employees need training on basic business practices, as well industry regulations and specific cannabis related skills. There is a huge shortage of training programs for cannabis employees. Many state regulations now are mandating employee-training courses, all but guaranteeing a built-in market for corporate education.

There are also opportunities to educate professionals like lawyers, doctors and nurses who are required to take continuing education courses. Many will likely select continuing education credit granting coursework in cannabis to learn more about the business.

After all, if you were a tax professional and had a choice to take a course, would you choose the latest arcane IRS regulations regarding depreciation, or a class on cannabis and taxes?

How can you start as an entrepreneur in this industry?

What are some ways that you can create jobs for others, or gain employment in the cannabis industry for experience?

How can you enter into the industry in compliance, what are some ways you can assist with regulation?

Feeling Excited?

Cannabis isn't the next big thing, it is now officially 'the thing'. It's the first new industry in the United States in a generation, and in four short years since Colorado became the first state to completely abolish prohibition, America's cannabis industry has mushroomed to an estimated 11 billion dollars annually---with continued double digit growth on the horizon. This is only the beginning. As more states legalize and more consumers join the movement, entrepreneurs who've founded businesses and people who transition into the industry now will be positioned to profit off of growing demand.

If you are even remotely interested in the cannabis industry, take the leap. Educate yourself about the plant, and the industry behind it. Expand on the foundation provided by this book. Take classes, like our cannabis master class, attend conferences, join associations, and read everything that you can get your hands on.

Think about your passions, skills and talents and how you can best apply them to a rapidly evolving market.

Opportunities like these don't come around very often and you owe it to yourself to fully explore this one. When I took the leap nearly three years ago, I had no idea what the future would hold, just a belief in myself and the importance of making the plant accessible to all people and the industry accessible to all communities, particularly those like mine, which has been devastated by America's war on drugs. It's been a whirlwind, filled with dizzying highs and lows, and even a brush with law enforcement, but I have absolutely no regrets about my journey.

I hope that you will connect with me on social media and follow my progress: www.theweedhead.com, FB: Dasheeda Dawson - The Weedhead, Twitter and Instagram. And, I hope that you will join me in the industry. Together we can forge a brighter more inclusive future for the cannabis community. Together, we can change the world.

Still Have Questions?

On Fridays, we host the open Ask Me Anything "AMA" forum for the CannaCurious with Roz McCarthy, Founder and CEO of Minorities for Medical Marijuana.

Any questions, ideas, information or resources you might have regarding the industry will be answered here.

Roz McCarthy is a unique force within the cannabis community precisely because she puts her money where her mouth is. Driven by 20-plus years of business expertise and her devotion for equity within the medical marijuana industry, McCarthy founded Minorities for Medical Marijuana (M4MM) in May 2016.

What was initially prompted by a series of personal tragedies has resulted in an active entrepreneurial community that is rapidly spreading across the country, and beyond.

Join us at https://cannatalk.jarviz.io

Published By

Nexem Inc dba J.A.R.V.I.Z. Project

350 W Dickens, #2

Chicago, IL 60614

Website: https://jarviz.io

Email: support@jarviz.io

© The WeedHead LLC & the J.A.R.V.I.Z. Project. All rights reserved.

Protected by copyright laws of the United States and international treaties.

No part of this publication in whole or in part may be copies, duplicated, reproduced or transmitted in any form or by any means, electronic or mechanical, including photocopying, recording, or by any information storage and retrieval system, without the express written permission from the publisher.

Copyright and other intellectual property laws protect these materials and any unauthorized reproduction or retransmission will constitute an infringement of copyright law.

Federal law provides severe civil and criminal penalties for the unauthorized reproduction, distribution, or exhibition of copyrighted materials. Penalties for criminal and statutory copyright infringement are set forth at 18 U.S.C. § 2319.

ISBN: 978-1-7329975-0-9

Brand Credits and Acknowledgement

All logos and images highlighted in this book are the ownership of brands and companies listed below.

*Minorities For Medical Marijuana PG **3**, Victoria's Secret PG **15**, Target Corporation PG **16**, Levi Strauss PG **23**, Discovery Channels "Weed Wars" PG **29**, The Pot Book PG **35**, Women Grow PG **36**, Cannagather PG **36**, DNA Genetics Pg **41**, Sensi Seed Pg **41**, Loompa Farms Pg **41**, Crockett Family Farms Pg **40**, Swamp Boys Seeds Pg **41**, Dark Heart Nursery PG **43**, LiveWell™ Colorado PG **43**, Steep Hill Labs PG **48**, Swami™ Select PG **50**, Marigold™ California PG **50**, Dr. Greenthumb PG **52**, LiveWell™ Colorado PG **52**, DragonFish PG **52**, High Latitude Farms PG **53**, Clean Green Certified™ PG **53**, Moxie PG **60**, Blue River Terps PG **60**, LoudPack PG **60**, Gold Drops Co. PG **60**, , Aunt Zelda's PG **65**, Ebbu LLC PG **65**, 1906 PG **65**, ViPova™ Tea PG **65**, Mary's Medicinals™ PG **70**, Dr. Green's PG **70**, Aunt Zelda's PG **70**, Dixie™ PG **70**, Kiva™ Confentions PG **70**, Bhang PG **70**, Altai Brands PG **70**, Mary's Medicinals™ PG **70**, BioTrack THC PG **86**, MJ Freeway PG **86**, Cannagather PG **85**, Cannabis Education Advocacy Symposuim & Expo - CEASE PG **85**, National Cannabis Festival PG **85**, Cannabis World Congress Business Exposition™ PG **85**, Estrohaze PG **80**, Leafly PG **80**, Weedmaps PG **80**, Sonia Gomez PG **88**, Charlo Green PG **88**, The Dank Duchess PG **88**, The WeedHead™ PG **88**, Julie PG **88**, 420 Goodybox PG **91**, Jayn Green PG **95***